THIS BOOK BELONGS TO :

_____

_____

WEEK AT A GLANCE

	MONDAY	TUESDAY	WEDNESDAY	THURSDAY	FRIDAY
✏️ GROUP :					
✏️ GROUP :					
✏️ GROUP :					
✏️ GROUP :					
✏️ GROUP :					

WEEK AT A GLANCE

	MONDAY	TUESDAY	WEDNESDAY	THURSDAY	FRIDAY
✏️ GROUP:					
✏️ GROUP:					
✏️ GROUP:					
✏️ GROUP:					
✏️ GROUP:					

WEEK AT A GLANCE

	MONDAY	TUESDAY	WEDNESDAY	THURSDAY	FRIDAY
✏ GROUP:					
✏ GROUP:					
✏ GROUP:					
✏ GROUP:					
✏ GROUP:					

WEEK AT A GLANCE

	MONDAY	TUESDAY	WEDNESDAY	THURSDAY	FRIDAY
✏️ GROUP :					
✏️ GROUP :					
✏️ GROUP :					
✏️ GROUP :					
✏️ GROUP :					

WEEK AT A GLANCE

	MONDAY	TUESDAY	WEDNESDAY	THURSDAY	FRIDAY
✏ GROUP :					
✏ GROUP :					
✏ GROUP :					
✏ GROUP :					
✏ GROUP :					

WEEK AT A GLANCE

	MONDAY	TUESDAY	WEDNESDAY	THURSDAY	FRIDAY
✏️ GROUP :					
✏️ GROUP :					
✏️ GROUP :					
✏️ GROUP :					
✏️ GROUP :					

WEEK AT A GLANCE

	MONDAY	TUESDAY	WEDNESDAY	THURSDAY	FRIDAY
✏ GROUP :					
✏ GROUP :					
✏ GROUP :					
✏ GROUP :					
✏ GROUP :					

WEEK AT A GLANCE

	MONDAY	TUESDAY	WEDNESDAY	THURSDAY	FRIDAY
✏️ GROUP :					
✏️ GROUP :					
✏️ GROUP :					
✏️ GROUP :					
✏️ GROUP :					

WEEK AT A GLANCE

	MONDAY	TUESDAY	WEDNESDAY	THURSDAY	FRIDAY
✏ GROUP :					
✏ GROUP :					
✏ GROUP :					
✏ GROUP :					
✏ GROUP :					

WEEK AT A GLANCE

	MONDAY	TUESDAY	WEDNESDAY	THURSDAY	FRIDAY
✏ GROUP :					
✏ GROUP :					
✏ GROUP :					
✏ GROUP :					
✏ GROUP :					

WEEK AT A GLANCE

	MONDAY	TUESDAY	WEDNESDAY	THURSDAY	FRIDAY
✎ GROUP :					
✎ GROUP :					
✎ GROUP :					
✎ GROUP :					
✎ GROUP :					

WEEK AT A GLANCE

	MONDAY	TUESDAY	WEDNESDAY	THURSDAY	FRIDAY
✏ GROUP:					
✏ GROUP:					
✏ GROUP:					
✏ GROUP:					
✏ GROUP:					

WEEK AT A GLANCE

	MONDAY	TUESDAY	WEDNESDAY	THURSDAY	FRIDAY
✏ GROUP:					
✏ GROUP:					
✏ GROUP:					
✏ GROUP:					
✏ GROUP:					

WEEK AT A GLANCE

	MONDAY	TUESDAY	WEDNESDAY	THURSDAY	FRIDAY
✏ GROUP :					
✏ GROUP :					
✏ GROUP :					
✏ GROUP :					
✏ GROUP :					

WEEK AT A GLANCE

	MONDAY	TUESDAY	WEDNESDAY	THURSDAY	FRIDAY
✏ GROUP:					
✏ GROUP:					
✏ GROUP:					
✏ GROUP:					
✏ GROUP:					

WEEK AT A GLANCE

	MONDAY	TUESDAY	WEDNESDAY	THURSDAY	FRIDAY
✏️ GROUP :					
✏️ GROUP :					
✏️ GROUP :					
✏️ GROUP :					
✏️ GROUP :					

WEEK AT A GLANCE

	MONDAY	TUESDAY	WEDNESDAY	THURSDAY	FRIDAY
✏ GROUP :					
✏ GROUP :					
✏ GROUP :					
✏ GROUP :					
✏ GROUP :					

WEEK AT A GLANCE

	MONDAY	TUESDAY	WEDNESDAY	THURSDAY	FRIDAY
✏️ GROUP :					
✏️ GROUP :					
✏️ GROUP :					
✏️ GROUP :					
✏️ GROUP :					

WEEK AT A GLANCE

	MONDAY	TUESDAY	WEDNESDAY	THURSDAY	FRIDAY
✏ GROUP :					
✏ GROUP :					
✏ GROUP :					
✏ GROUP :					
✏ GROUP :					

WEEK AT A GLANCE

	MONDAY	TUESDAY	WEDNESDAY	THURSDAY	FRIDAY
✎ GROUP :					
✎ GROUP :					
✎ GROUP :					
✎ GROUP :					
✎ GROUP :					

GUIDED READING PLANBOOK

DATE: GROUP:

BOOK TITLE: LEVEL:

✏ BOOK INTRODUCTION:

✏ WORD WORK: ✏ VOCABULARY:

✏ TEACHING STRATEGY:

✏ BEFORE READING:

✏ DURING READING:

✏ AFTER READING:

✏ NOTES:

GUIDED READING OBSERVATION NOTES

DATE:
GROUP:

NAMES OF STUDENTS

BEFORE READING					
MAKES PREDICTIONS					
NOTICES NEW WORDS					
RECOGNISES SIGHT WORDS					
SCANS TEXT FOR CLUES					
SCANS IMAGES FOR CLUES					
DURING READING					
APPLIES STRATEGIES FOR NEW WORDS					
READS FLUENTLY					
SELF-CORRECTS					
RE-READS FOR MEANING					
AFTER READING					
IDENTIFIES MAIN IDEAS					
SUMMARIZES TOPIC IN ONE SENTENCE					
RECALLS EVENTS IN PROPER ORDER					
RETELLS TEXT ACCURATELY					

NOTES

GUIDED READING PLANBOOK

DATE:
BOOK TITLE:

GROUP:
LEVEL:

✏ BOOK INTRODUCTION:

✏ WORD WORK:

✏ VOCABULARY:

✏ TEACHING STRATEGY:

✏ BEFORE READING:

✏ DURING READING:

✏ AFTER READING:

✏ NOTES:

GUIDED READING OBSERVATION NOTES

DATE:
GROUP:

	NAMES OF STUDENTS				
BEFORE READING					
MAKES PREDICTIONS					
NOTICES NEW WORDS					
RECOGNISES SIGHT WORDS					
SCANS TEXT FOR CLUES					
SCANS IMAGES FOR CLUES					
DURING READING					
APPLIES STRATEGIES FOR NEW WORDS					
READS FLUENTLY					
SELF-CORRECTS					
RE-READS FOR MEANING					
AFTER READING					
IDENTIFIES MAIN IDEAS					
SUMMARIZES TOPIC IN ONE SENTENCE					
RECALLS EVENTS IN PROPER ORDER					
RETELLS TEXT ACCURATELY					
NOTES					

GUIDED READING PLANBOOK

DATE: _____ GROUP: _____
BOOK TITLE: _____ LEVEL: _____

✏ BOOK INTRODUCTION:

✏ WORD WORK:	✏ VOCABULARY:

✏ TEACHING STRATEGY:

✏ BEFORE READING:

✏ DURING READING:

✏ AFTER READING:

✏ NOTES:

GUIDED READING OBSERVATION NOTES

DATE:
GROUP:

	NAMES OF STUDENTS				
BEFORE READING					
MAKES PREDICTIONS					
NOTICES NEW WORDS					
RECOGNISES SIGHT WORDS					
SCANS TEXT FOR CLUES					
SCANS IMAGES FOR CLUES					
DURING READING					
APPLIES STRATEGIES FOR NEW WORDS					
READS FLUENTLY					
SELF-CORRECTS					
RE-READS FOR MEANING					
AFTER READING					
IDENTIFIES MAIN IDEAS					
SUMMARIZES TOPIC IN ONE SENTENCE					
RECALLS EVENTS IN PROPER ORDER					
RETELLS TEXT ACCURATELY					
NOTES					

GUIDED READING PLANBOOK

DATE: GROUP:

BOOK TITLE: LEVEL:

✏ BOOK INTRODUCTION:

✏ WORD WORK: ✏ VOCABULARY:

✏ TEACHING STRATEGY:

✏ BEFORE READING:

✏ DURING READING:

✏ AFTER READING:

✏ NOTES:

GUIDED READING OBSERVATION NOTES

DATE:
GROUP:

NAMES OF STUDENTS

BEFORE READING	MAKES PREDICTIONS					
	NOTICES NEW WORDS					
	RECOGNISES SIGHT WORDS					
	SCANS TEXT FOR CLUES					
	SCANS IMAGES FOR CLUES					
DURING READING	APPLIES STRATEGIES FOR NEW WORDS					
	READS FLUENTLY					
	SELF-CORRECTS					
	RE-READS FOR MEANING					
AFTER READING	IDENTIFIES MAIN IDEAS					
	SUMMARIZES TOPIC IN ONE SENTENCE					
	RECALLS EVENTS IN PROPER ORDER					
	RETELLS TEXT ACCURATELY					

NOTES

GUIDED READING PLANBOOK

DATE:
BOOK TITLE:

GROUP:
LEVEL:

✏ BOOK INTRODUCTION:

✏ WORD WORK:

✏ VOCABULARY:

✏ TEACHING STRATEGY:

✏ BEFORE READING:

✏ DURING READING:

✏ AFTER READING:

✏ NOTES:

GUIDED READING OBSERVATION NOTES

DATE:
GROUP:

	NAMES OF STUDENTS				

BEFORE READING						
MAKES PREDICTIONS						
NOTICES NEW WORDS						
RECOGNISES SIGHT WORDS						
SCANS TEXT FOR CLUES						
SCANS IMAGES FOR CLUES						

DURING READING						
APPLIES STRATEGIES FOR NEW WORDS						
READS FLUENTLY						
SELF-CORRECTS						
RE-READS FOR MEANING						

AFTER READING						
IDENTIFIES MAIN IDEAS						
SUMMARIZES TOPIC IN ONE SENTENCE						
RECALLS EVENTS IN PROPER ORDER						
RETELLS TEXT ACCURATELY						

NOTES

GUIDED READING PLANBOOK

DATE:
BOOK TITLE:

GROUP:
LEVEL:

✏ BOOK INTRODUCTION:

✏ WORD WORK:

✏ VOCABULARY:

✏ TEACHING STRATEGY:

✏ BEFORE READING:

✏ DURING READING:

✏ AFTER READING:

✏ NOTES:

GUIDED READING OBSERVATION NOTES

DATE:
GROUP:

NAMES OF STUDENTS

BEFORE READING	MAKES PREDICTIONS					
	NOTICES NEW WORDS					
	RECOGNISES SIGHT WORDS					
	SCANS TEXT FOR CLUES					
	SCANS IMAGES FOR CLUES					
DURING READING	APPLIES STRATEGIES FOR NEW WORDS					
	READS FLUENTLY					
	SELF-CORRECTS					
	RE-READS FOR MEANING					
AFTER READING	IDENTIFIES MAIN IDEAS					
	SUMMARIZES TOPIC IN ONE SENTENCE					
	RECALLS EVENTS IN PROPER ORDER					
	RETELLS TEXT ACCURATELY					

NOTES

GUIDED READING PLANBOOK

DATE:
BOOK TITLE:

GROUP:
LEVEL:

✏ BOOK INTRODUCTION:

✏ WORD WORK:

✏ VOCABULARY:

✏ TEACHING STRATEGY:

✏ BEFORE READING:

✏ DURING READING:

✏ AFTER READING:

✏ NOTES:

GUIDED READING OBSERVATION NOTES

DATE:
GROUP:

	NAMES OF STUDENTS				
BEFORE READING					
MAKES PREDICTIONS					
NOTICES NEW WORDS					
RECOGNISES SIGHT WORDS					
SCANS TEXT FOR CLUES					
SCANS IMAGES FOR CLUES					
DURING READING					
APPLIES STRATEGIES FOR NEW WORDS					
READS FLUENTLY					
SELF-CORRECTS					
RE-READS FOR MEANING					
AFTER READING					
IDENTIFIES MAIN IDEAS					
SUMMARIZES TOPIC IN ONE SENTENCE					
RECALLS EVENTS IN PROPER ORDER					
RETELLS TEXT ACCURATELY					

NOTES

GUIDED READING PLANBOOK

DATE:

BOOK TITLE:

GROUP:

LEVEL:

✏ BOOK INTRODUCTION:

✏ WORD WORK: | ✏ VOCABULARY:

✏ TEACHING STRATEGY:

✏ BEFORE READING:

✏ DURING READING:

✏ AFTER READING:

✏ NOTES:

GUIDED READING OBSERVATION NOTES

DATE:
GROUP:

		NAMES OF STUDENTS				
BEFORE READING	MAKES PREDICTIONS					
	NOTICES NEW WORDS					
	RECOGNISES SIGHT WORDS					
	SCANS TEXT FOR CLUES					
	SCANS IMAGES FOR CLUES					
DURING READING	APPLIES STRATEGIES FOR NEW WORDS					
	READS FLUENTLY					
	SELF-CORRECTS					
	RE-READS FOR MEANING					
AFTER READING	IDENTIFIES MAIN IDEAS					
	SUMMARIZES TOPIC IN ONE SENTENCE					
	RECALLS EVENTS IN PROPER ORDER					
	RETELLS TEXT ACCURATELY					
NOTES						

GUIDED READING PLANBOOK

DATE: GROUP:

BOOK TITLE: LEVEL:

✏ BOOK INTRODUCTION:

✏ WORD WORK: ✏ VOCABULARY:

✏ TEACHING STRATEGY:

✏ BEFORE READING:

✏ DURING READING:

✏ AFTER READING:

✏ NOTES:

GUIDED READING OBSERVATION NOTES

DATE:
GROUP:

	NAMES OF STUDENTS				
BEFORE READING					
MAKES PREDICTIONS					
NOTICES NEW WORDS					
RECOGNISES SIGHT WORDS					
SCANS TEXT FOR CLUES					
SCANS IMAGES FOR CLUES					
DURING READING					
APPLIES STRATEGIES FOR NEW WORDS					
READS FLUENTLY					
SELF-CORRECTS					
RE-READS FOR MEANING					
AFTER READING					
IDENTIFIES MAIN IDEAS					
SUMMARIZES TOPIC IN ONE SENTENCE					
RECALLS EVENTS IN PROPER ORDER					
RETELLS TEXT ACCURATELY					
NOTES					

GUIDED READING PLANBOOK

DATE: GROUP:

BOOK TITLE: LEVEL:

✏ BOOK INTRODUCTION:

✏ WORD WORK: ✏ VOCABULARY:

✏ TEACHING STRATEGY:

✏ BEFORE READING:

✏ DURING READING:

✏ AFTER READING:

✏ NOTES:

GUIDED READING OBSERVATION NOTES

DATE:
GROUP:

		NAMES OF STUDENTS				
BEFORE READING	MAKES PREDICTIONS					
	NOTICES NEW WORDS					
	RECOGNISES SIGHT WORDS					
	SCANS TEXT FOR CLUES					
	SCANS IMAGES FOR CLUES					
DURING READING	APPLIES STRATEGIES FOR NEW WORDS					
	READS FLUENTLY					
	SELF-CORRECTS					
	RE-READS FOR MEANING					
AFTER READING	IDENTIFIES MAIN IDEAS					
	SUMMARIZES TOPIC IN ONE SENTENCE					
	RECALLS EVENTS IN PROPER ORDER					
	RETELLS TEXT ACCURATELY					
NOTES						

GUIDED READING PLANBOOK

DATE: GROUP:

BOOK TITLE: LEVEL:

BOOK INTRODUCTION:

WORD WORK: | VOCABULARY:

TEACHING STRATEGY:

BEFORE READING:

DURING READING:

AFTER READING:

NOTES:

GUIDED READING OBSERVATION NOTES

DATE:
GROUP:

	NAMES OF STUDENTS				
BEFORE READING					
MAKES PREDICTIONS					
NOTICES NEW WORDS					
RECOGNISES SIGHT WORDS					
SCANS TEXT FOR CLUES					
SCANS IMAGES FOR CLUES					
DURING READING					
APPLIES STRATEGIES FOR NEW WORDS					
READS FLUENTLY					
SELF-CORRECTS					
RE-READS FOR MEANING					
AFTER READING					
IDENTIFIES MAIN IDEAS					
SUMMARIZES TOPIC IN ONE SENTENCE					
RECALLS EVENTS IN PROPER ORDER					
RETELLS TEXT ACCURATELY					
NOTES					

GUIDED READING PLANBOOK

DATE:
BOOK TITLE:

GROUP:
LEVEL:

✏ BOOK INTRODUCTION:

✏ WORD WORK:

✏ VOCABULARY:

✏ TEACHING STRATEGY:

✏ BEFORE READING:

✏ DURING READING:

✏ AFTER READING:

✏ NOTES:

GUIDED READING OBSERVATION NOTES

DATE:
GROUP:

		NAMES OF STUDENTS				
BEFORE READING	MAKES PREDICTIONS					
	NOTICES NEW WORDS					
	RECOGNISES SIGHT WORDS					
	SCANS TEXT FOR CLUES					
	SCANS IMAGES FOR CLUES					
DURING READING	APPLIES STRATEGIES FOR NEW WORDS					
	READS FLUENTLY					
	SELF-CORRECTS					
	RE-READS FOR MEANING					
AFTER READING	IDENTIFIES MAIN IDEAS					
	SUMMARIZES TOPIC IN ONE SENTENCE					
	RECALLS EVENTS IN PROPER ORDER					
	RETELLS TEXT ACCURATELY					
NOTES						

GUIDED READING PLANBOOK

DATE:
BOOK TITLE:

GROUP:
LEVEL:

✏ BOOK INTRODUCTION:

✏ WORD WORK: | ✏ VOCABULARY:

✏ TEACHING STRATEGY:

✏ BEFORE READING:

✏ DURING READING:

✏ AFTER READING:

✏ NOTES:

GUIDED READING OBSERVATION NOTES

DATE:
GROUP:

NAMES OF STUDENTS

BEFORE READING	MAKES PREDICTIONS					
	NOTICES NEW WORDS					
	RECOGNISES SIGHT WORDS					
	SCANS TEXT FOR CLUES					
	SCANS IMAGES FOR CLUES					
DURING READING	APPLIES STRATEGIES FOR NEW WORDS					
	READS FLUENTLY					
	SELF-CORRECTS					
	RE-READS FOR MEANING					
AFTER READING	IDENTIFIES MAIN IDEAS					
	SUMMARIZES TOPIC IN ONE SENTENCE					
	RECALLS EVENTS IN PROPER ORDER					
	RETELLS TEXT ACCURATELY					

NOTES

GUIDED READING PLANBOOK

DATE:
BOOK TITLE:

GROUP:
LEVEL:

✏ BOOK INTRODUCTION:

✏ WORD WORK:

✏ VOCABULARY:

✏ TEACHING STRATEGY:

✏ BEFORE READING:

✏ DURING READING:

✏ AFTER READING:

✏ NOTES:

GUIDED READING OBSERVATION NOTES

DATE:
GROUP:

		NAMES OF STUDENTS				
BEFORE READING	MAKES PREDICTIONS					
	NOTICES NEW WORDS					
	RECOGNISES SIGHT WORDS					
	SCANS TEXT FOR CLUES					
	SCANS IMAGES FOR CLUES					
DURING READING	APPLIES STRATEGIES FOR NEW WORDS					
	READS FLUENTLY					
	SELF-CORRECTS					
	RE-READS FOR MEANING					
AFTER READING	IDENTIFIES MAIN IDEAS					
	SUMMARIZES TOPIC IN ONE SENTENCE					
	RECALLS EVENTS IN PROPER ORDER					
	RETELLS TEXT ACCURATELY					
NOTES						

GUIDED READING PLANBOOK

DATE:
BOOK TITLE:

GROUP:
LEVEL:

BOOK INTRODUCTION:

WORD WORK:

VOCABULARY:

TEACHING STRATEGY:

BEFORE READING:

DURING READING:

AFTER READING:

NOTES:

GUIDED READING OBSERVATION NOTES

DATE:
GROUP:

		NAMES OF STUDENTS				
BEFORE READING	MAKES PREDICTIONS					
	NOTICES NEW WORDS					
	RECOGNISES SIGHT WORDS					
	SCANS TEXT FOR CLUES					
	SCANS IMAGES FOR CLUES					
DURING READING	APPLIES STRATEGIES FOR NEW WORDS					
	READS FLUENTLY					
	SELF-CORRECTS					
	RE-READS FOR MEANING					
AFTER READING	IDENTIFIES MAIN IDEAS					
	SUMMARIZES TOPIC IN ONE SENTENCE					
	RECALLS EVENTS IN PROPER ORDER					
	RETELLS TEXT ACCURATELY					
NOTES						

GUIDED READING PLANBOOK

DATE: GROUP:

BOOK TITLE: LEVEL:

BOOK INTRODUCTION:

WORD WORK: VOCABULARY:

TEACHING STRATEGY:

BEFORE READING:

DURING READING:

AFTER READING:

NOTES:

GUIDED READING OBSERVATION NOTES

DATE:
GROUP:

NAMES OF STUDENTS

BEFORE READING					
MAKES PREDICTIONS					
NOTICES NEW WORDS					
RECOGNISES SIGHT WORDS					
SCANS TEXT FOR CLUES					
SCANS IMAGES FOR CLUES					
DURING READING					
APPLIES STRATEGIES FOR NEW WORDS					
READS FLUENTLY					
SELF-CORRECTS					
RE-READS FOR MEANING					
AFTER READING					
IDENTIFIES MAIN IDEAS					
SUMMARIZES TOPIC IN ONE SENTENCE					
RECALLS EVENTS IN PROPER ORDER					
RETELLS TEXT ACCURATELY					
NOTES					

GUIDED READING PLANBOOK

DATE: GROUP:

BOOK TITLE: LEVEL:

✏ BOOK INTRODUCTION:

✏ WORD WORK: ✏ VOCABULARY:

✏ TEACHING STRATEGY:

✏ BEFORE READING:

✏ DURING READING:

✏ AFTER READING:

✏ NOTES:

GUIDED READING OBSERVATION NOTES

DATE:
GROUP:

NAMES OF STUDENTS

BEFORE READING					
MAKES PREDICTIONS					
NOTICES NEW WORDS					
RECOGNISES SIGHT WORDS					
SCANS TEXT FOR CLUES					
SCANS IMAGES FOR CLUES					
DURING READING					
APPLIES STRATEGIES FOR NEW WORDS					
READS FLUENTLY					
SELF-CORRECTS					
RE-READS FOR MEANING					
AFTER READING					
IDENTIFIES MAIN IDEAS					
SUMMARIZES TOPIC IN ONE SENTENCE					
RECALLS EVENTS IN PROPER ORDER					
RETELLS TEXT ACCURATELY					

NOTES

GUIDED READING PLANBOOK

DATE: GROUP:

BOOK TITLE: LEVEL:

✏ BOOK INTRODUCTION:

✏ WORD WORK: ✏ VOCABULARY:

✏ TEACHING STRATEGY:

✏ BEFORE READING:

✏ DURING READING:

✏ AFTER READING:

✏ NOTES:

GUIDED READING OBSERVATION NOTES

DATE:
GROUP:

NAMES OF STUDENTS

BEFORE READING
- MAKES PREDICTIONS
- NOTICES NEW WORDS
- RECOGNISES SIGHT WORDS
- SCANS TEXT FOR CLUES
- SCANS IMAGES FOR CLUES

DURING READING
- APPLIES STRATEGIES FOR NEW WORDS
- READS FLUENTLY
- SELF-CORRECTS
- RE-READS FOR MEANING

AFTER READING
- IDENTIFIES MAIN IDEAS
- SUMMARIZES TOPIC IN ONE SENTENCE
- RECALLS EVENTS IN PROPER ORDER
- RETELLS TEXT ACCURATELY

NOTES

GUIDED READING PLANBOOK

DATE: GROUP:

BOOK TITLE: LEVEL:

✏ BOOK INTRODUCTION:

✏ WORD WORK: ✏ VOCABULARY:

✏ TEACHING STRATEGY:

✏ BEFORE READING:

✏ DURING READING:

✏ AFTER READING:

✏ NOTES:

GUIDED READING OBSERVATION NOTES

DATE:
GROUP:

	NAMES OF STUDENTS				

BEFORE READING						
	MAKES PREDICTIONS					
	NOTICES NEW WORDS					
	RECOGNISES SIGHT WORDS					
	SCANS TEXT FOR CLUES					
	SCANS IMAGES FOR CLUES					

DURING READING						
	APPLIES STRATEGIES FOR NEW WORDS					
	READS FLUENTLY					
	SELF-CORRECTS					
	RE-READS FOR MEANING					

AFTER READING						
	IDENTIFIES MAIN IDEAS					
	SUMMARIZES TOPIC IN ONE SENTENCE					
	RECALLS EVENTS IN PROPER ORDER					
	RETELLS TEXT ACCURATELY					

NOTES					

GUIDED READING PLANBOOK

DATE:

GROUP:

BOOK TITLE:

LEVEL:

✎ BOOK INTRODUCTION:

✎ WORD WORK:

✎ VOCABULARY:

✎ TEACHING STRATEGY:

✎ BEFORE READING:

✎ DURING READING:

✎ AFTER READING:

✎ NOTES:

GUIDED READING OBSERVATION NOTES

DATE:
GROUP:

		NAMES OF STUDENTS				
BEFORE READING	MAKES PREDICTIONS					
	NOTICES NEW WORDS					
	RECOGNISES SIGHT WORDS					
	SCANS TEXT FOR CLUES					
	SCANS IMAGES FOR CLUES					
DURING READING	APPLIES STRATEGIES FOR NEW WORDS					
	READS FLUENTLY					
	SELF-CORRECTS					
	RE-READS FOR MEANING					
AFTER READING	IDENTIFIES MAIN IDEAS					
	SUMMARIZES TOPIC IN ONE SENTENCE					
	RECALLS EVENTS IN PROPER ORDER					
	RETELLS TEXT ACCURATELY					
	NOTES					

GUIDED READING PLANBOOK

DATE:

BOOK TITLE:

GROUP:

LEVEL:

✎ BOOK INTRODUCTION:

✎ WORD WORK:

✎ VOCABULARY:

✎ TEACHING STRATEGY:

✎ BEFORE READING:

✎ DURING READING:

✎ AFTER READING:

✎ NOTES:

GUIDED READING OBSERVATION NOTES

DATE:
GROUP:

		NAMES OF STUDENTS				
BEFORE READING	MAKES PREDICTIONS					
	NOTICES NEW WORDS					
	RECOGNISES SIGHT WORDS					
	SCANS TEXT FOR CLUES					
	SCANS IMAGES FOR CLUES					
DURING READING	APPLIES STRATEGIES FOR NEW WORDS					
	READS FLUENTLY					
	SELF-CORRECTS					
	RE-READS FOR MEANING					
AFTER READING	IDENTIFIES MAIN IDEAS					
	SUMMARIZES TOPIC IN ONE SENTENCE					
	RECALLS EVENTS IN PROPER ORDER					
	RETELLS TEXT ACCURATELY					
NOTES						

GUIDED READING PLANBOOK

DATE:
BOOK TITLE:

GROUP:
LEVEL:

✏ BOOK INTRODUCTION:

✏ WORD WORK: | ✏ VOCABULARY:

✏ TEACHING STRATEGY:

✏ BEFORE READING:

✏ DURING READING:

✏ AFTER READING:

✏ NOTES:

GUIDED READING OBSERVATION NOTES

DATE:
GROUP:

		NAMES OF STUDENTS				
BEFORE READING	MAKES PREDICTIONS					
	NOTICES NEW WORDS					
	RECOGNISES SIGHT WORDS					
	SCANS TEXT FOR CLUES					
	SCANS IMAGES FOR CLUES					
DURING READING	APPLIES STRATEGIES FOR NEW WORDS					
	READS FLUENTLY					
	SELF-CORRECTS					
	RE-READS FOR MEANING					
AFTER READING	IDENTIFIES MAIN IDEAS					
	SUMMARIZES TOPIC IN ONE SENTENCE					
	RECALLS EVENTS IN PROPER ORDER					
	RETELLS TEXT ACCURATELY					
	NOTES					

GUIDED READING PLANBOOK

DATE: GROUP:
BOOK TITLE: LEVEL:

✏ BOOK INTRODUCTION:

✏ WORD WORK: ✏ VOCABULARY:

✏ TEACHING STRATEGY:

✏ BEFORE READING:

✏ DURING READING:

✏ AFTER READING:

✏ NOTES:

GUIDED READING OBSERVATION NOTES

DATE:
GROUP:

		NAMES OF STUDENTS				
BEFORE READING	MAKES PREDICTIONS					
	NOTICES NEW WORDS					
	RECOGNISES SIGHT WORDS					
	SCANS TEXT FOR CLUES					
	SCANS IMAGES FOR CLUES					
DURING READING	APPLIES STRATEGIES FOR NEW WORDS					
	READS FLUENTLY					
	SELF-CORRECTS					
	RE-READS FOR MEANING					
AFTER READING	IDENTIFIES MAIN IDEAS					
	SUMMARIZES TOPIC IN ONE SENTENCE					
	RECALLS EVENTS IN PROPER ORDER					
	RETELLS TEXT ACCURATELY					
NOTES						

GUIDED READING PLANBOOK

DATE: GROUP:

BOOK TITLE: LEVEL:

BOOK INTRODUCTION:

WORD WORK: VOCABULARY:

TEACHING STRATEGY:

BEFORE READING:

DURING READING:

AFTER READING:

NOTES:

GUIDED READING OBSERVATION NOTES

		NAMES OF STUDENTS				
DATE: GROUP:						
BEFORE READING	MAKES PREDICTIONS					
	NOTICES NEW WORDS					
	RECOGNISES SIGHT WORDS					
	SCANS TEXT FOR CLUES					
	SCANS IMAGES FOR CLUES					
DURING READING	APPLIES STRATEGIES FOR NEW WORDS					
	READS FLUENTLY					
	SELF-CORRECTS					
	RE-READS FOR MEANING					
AFTER READING	IDENTIFIES MAIN IDEAS					
	SUMMARIZES TOPIC IN ONE SENTENCE					
	RECALLS EVENTS IN PROPER ORDER					
	RETELLS TEXT ACCURATELY					
NOTES						

GUIDED READING PLANBOOK

DATE: GROUP:

BOOK TITLE: LEVEL:

✏ BOOK INTRODUCTION:

✏ WORD WORK: ✏ VOCABULARY:

✏ TEACHING STRATEGY:

✏ BEFORE READING:

✏ DURING READING:

✏ AFTER READING:

✏ NOTES:

GUIDED READING OBSERVATION NOTES

DATE:
GROUP:

NAMES OF STUDENTS

BEFORE READING	MAKES PREDICTIONS					
	NOTICES NEW WORDS					
	RECOGNISES SIGHT WORDS					
	SCANS TEXT FOR CLUES					
	SCANS IMAGES FOR CLUES					
DURING READING	APPLIES STRATEGIES FOR NEW WORDS					
	READS FLUENTLY					
	SELF-CORRECTS					
	RE-READS FOR MEANING					
AFTER READING	IDENTIFIES MAIN IDEAS					
	SUMMARIZES TOPIC IN ONE SENTENCE					
	RECALLS EVENTS IN PROPER ORDER					
	RETELLS TEXT ACCURATELY					
NOTES						

GUIDED READING PLANBOOK

DATE: GROUP:
BOOK TITLE: LEVEL:

✏ BOOK INTRODUCTION:

✏ WORD WORK: ✏ VOCABULARY:

✏ TEACHING STRATEGY:

✏ BEFORE READING:

✏ DURING READING:

✏ AFTER READING:

✏ NOTES:

GUIDED READING OBSERVATION NOTES

DATE:
GROUP:

		NAMES OF STUDENTS				
BEFORE READING	MAKES PREDICTIONS					
	NOTICES NEW WORDS					
	RECOGNISES SIGHT WORDS					
	SCANS TEXT FOR CLUES					
	SCANS IMAGES FOR CLUES					
DURING READING	APPLIES STRATEGIES FOR NEW WORDS					
	READS FLUENTLY					
	SELF-CORRECTS					
	RE-READS FOR MEANING					
AFTER READING	IDENTIFIES MAIN IDEAS					
	SUMMARIZES TOPIC IN ONE SENTENCE					
	RECALLS EVENTS IN PROPER ORDER					
	RETELLS TEXT ACCURATELY					
NOTES						

GUIDED READING PLANBOOK

DATE:
BOOK TITLE:

GROUP:
LEVEL:

✏ BOOK INTRODUCTION:

✏ WORD WORK:

✏ VOCABULARY:

✏ TEACHING STRATEGY:

✏ BEFORE READING:

✏ DURING READING:

✏ AFTER READING:

✏ NOTES:

GUIDED READING OBSERVATION NOTES

DATE:
GROUP:

		NAMES OF STUDENTS				
BEFORE READING	MAKES PREDICTIONS					
	NOTICES NEW WORDS					
	RECOGNISES SIGHT WORDS					
	SCANS TEXT FOR CLUES					
	SCANS IMAGES FOR CLUES					
DURING READING	APPLIES STRATEGIES FOR NEW WORDS					
	READS FLUENTLY					
	SELF-CORRECTS					
	RE-READS FOR MEANING					
AFTER READING	IDENTIFIES MAIN IDEAS					
	SUMMARIZES TOPIC IN ONE SENTENCE					
	RECALLS EVENTS IN PROPER ORDER					
	RETELLS TEXT ACCURATELY					

NOTES

GUIDED READING PLANBOOK

DATE: GROUP:

BOOK TITLE: LEVEL:

✏ BOOK INTRODUCTION:

✏ WORD WORK: ✏ VOCABULARY:

✏ TEACHING STRATEGY:

✏ BEFORE READING:

✏ DURING READING:

✏ AFTER READING:

✏ NOTES:

GUIDED READING OBSERVATION NOTES

DATE:
GROUP:

		NAMES OF STUDENTS				
BEFORE READING	MAKES PREDICTIONS					
	NOTICES NEW WORDS					
	RECOGNISES SIGHT WORDS					
	SCANS TEXT FOR CLUES					
	SCANS IMAGES FOR CLUES					
DURING READING	APPLIES STRATEGIES FOR NEW WORDS					
	READS FLUENTLY					
	SELF-CORRECTS					
	RE-READS FOR MEANING					
AFTER READING	IDENTIFIES MAIN IDEAS					
	SUMMARIZES TOPIC IN ONE SENTENCE					
	RECALLS EVENTS IN PROPER ORDER					
	RETELLS TEXT ACCURATELY					
NOTES						

GUiDED READiNG PLANBOOK

DATE: GROUP:

BOOK TiTLE: LEVEL:

✏ BOOK iNTRODUCTiON:

✏ WORD WORK: ✏ VOCABULARY:

✏ TEACHiNG STRATEGY:

✏ BEFORE READiNG:

✏ DURiNG READiNG:

✏ AFTER READiNG:

✏ NOTES:

GUIDED READING OBSERVATION NOTES

DATE:
GROUP:

		NAMES OF STUDENTS				
BEFORE READING	MAKES PREDICTIONS					
	NOTICES NEW WORDS					
	RECOGNISES SIGHT WORDS					
	SCANS TEXT FOR CLUES					
	SCANS IMAGES FOR CLUES					
DURING READING	APPLIES STRATEGIES FOR NEW WORDS					
	READS FLUENTLY					
	SELF-CORRECTS					
	RE-READS FOR MEANING					
AFTER READING	IDENTIFIES MAIN IDEAS					
	SUMMARIZES TOPIC IN ONE SENTENCE					
	RECALLS EVENTS IN PROPER ORDER					
	RETELLS TEXT ACCURATELY					
NOTES						

GUIDED READING PLANBOOK

DATE: GROUP:

BOOK TITLE: LEVEL:

✏ BOOK INTRODUCTION:

✏ WORD WORK: **✏ VOCABULARY:**

✏ TEACHING STRATEGY:

✏ BEFORE READING:

✏ DURING READING:

✏ AFTER READING:

✏ NOTES:

GUIDED READING OBSERVATION NOTES

DATE:
GROUP:

		NAMES OF STUDENTS				
BEFORE READING	MAKES PREDICTIONS					
	NOTICES NEW WORDS					
	RECOGNISES SIGHT WORDS					
	SCANS TEXT FOR CLUES					
	SCANS IMAGES FOR CLUES					
DURING READING	APPLIES STRATEGIES FOR NEW WORDS					
	READS FLUENTLY					
	SELF-CORRECTS					
	RE-READS FOR MEANING					
AFTER READING	IDENTIFIES MAIN IDEAS					
	SUMMARIZES TOPIC IN ONE SENTENCE					
	RECALLS EVENTS IN PROPER ORDER					
	RETELLS TEXT ACCURATELY					
NOTES						

GUIDED READING PLANBOOK

DATE: GROUP:

BOOK TITLE: LEVEL:

✎ BOOK INTRODUCTION:

✎ WORD WORK: ✎ VOCABULARY:

✎ TEACHING STRATEGY:

✎ BEFORE READING:

✎ DURING READING:

✎ AFTER READING:

✎ NOTES:

GUIDED READING OBSERVATION NOTES

DATE:
GROUP:

	NAMES OF STUDENTS				
BEFORE READING					
MAKES PREDICTIONS					
NOTICES NEW WORDS					
RECOGNISES SIGHT WORDS					
SCANS TEXT FOR CLUES					
SCANS IMAGES FOR CLUES					
DURING READING					
APPLIES STRATEGIES FOR NEW WORDS					
READS FLUENTLY					
SELF-CORRECTS					
RE-READS FOR MEANING					
AFTER READING					
IDENTIFIES MAIN IDEAS					
SUMMARIZES TOPIC IN ONE SENTENCE					
RECALLS EVENTS IN PROPER ORDER					
RETELLS TEXT ACCURATELY					
NOTES					

GUIDED READING PLANBOOK

DATE: GROUP:

BOOK TITLE: LEVEL:

✏ BOOK INTRODUCTION:

✏ WORD WORK: ✏ VOCABULARY:

✏ TEACHING STRATEGY:

✏ BEFORE READING:

✏ DURING READING:

✏ AFTER READING:

✏ NOTES:

GUIDED READING OBSERVATION NOTES

DATE:
GROUP:

	NAMES OF STUDENTS				
BEFORE READING					
MAKES PREDICTIONS					
NOTICES NEW WORDS					
RECOGNISES SIGHT WORDS					
SCANS TEXT FOR CLUES					
SCANS IMAGES FOR CLUES					
DURING READING					
APPLIES STRATEGIES FOR NEW WORDS					
READS FLUENTLY					
SELF-CORRECTS					
RE-READS FOR MEANING					
AFTER READING					
IDENTIFIES MAIN IDEAS					
SUMMARIZES TOPIC IN ONE SENTENCE					
RECALLS EVENTS IN PROPER ORDER					
RETELLS TEXT ACCURATELY					
NOTES					

GUIDED READING PLANBOOK

DATE: | GROUP:
BOOK TITLE: | LEVEL:

✏ BOOK INTRODUCTION:

✏ WORD WORK: | ✏ VOCABULARY:

✏ TEACHING STRATEGY:

✏ BEFORE READING:

✏ DURING READING:

✏ AFTER READING:

✏ NOTES:

GUIDED READING OBSERVATION NOTES

DATE:
GROUP:

NAMES OF STUDENTS

BEFORE READING	MAKES PREDICTIONS					
	NOTICES NEW WORDS					
	RECOGNISES SIGHT WORDS					
	SCANS TEXT FOR CLUES					
	SCANS IMAGES FOR CLUES					
DURING READING	APPLIES STRATEGIES FOR NEW WORDS					
	READS FLUENTLY					
	SELF-CORRECTS					
	RE-READS FOR MEANING					
AFTER READING	IDENTIFIES MAIN IDEAS					
	SUMMARIZES TOPIC IN ONE SENTENCE					
	RECALLS EVENTS IN PROPER ORDER					
	RETELLS TEXT ACCURATELY					

NOTES

GUIDED READING PLANBOOK

DATE: GROUP:

BOOK TITLE: LEVEL:

✏ BOOK INTRODUCTION:

✏ WORD WORK: ✏ VOCABULARY:

✏ TEACHING STRATEGY:

✏ BEFORE READING:

✏ DURING READING:

✏ AFTER READING:

✏ NOTES:

GUIDED READING OBSERVATION NOTES

DATE:
GROUP:

		NAMES OF STUDENTS				
BEFORE READING	MAKES PREDICTIONS					
	NOTICES NEW WORDS					
	RECOGNISES SIGHT WORDS					
	SCANS TEXT FOR CLUES					
	SCANS IMAGES FOR CLUES					
DURING READING	APPLIES STRATEGIES FOR NEW WORDS					
	READS FLUENTLY					
	SELF-CORRECTS					
	RE-READS FOR MEANING					
AFTER READING	IDENTIFIES MAIN IDEAS					
	SUMMARIZES TOPIC IN ONE SENTENCE					
	RECALLS EVENTS IN PROPER ORDER					
	RETELLS TEXT ACCURATELY					
NOTES						

GUIDED READING PLANBOOK

DATE: GROUP:

BOOK TITLE: LEVEL:

✏ BOOK INTRODUCTION:

✏ WORD WORK: ✏ VOCABULARY:

✏ TEACHING STRATEGY:

✏ BEFORE READING:

✏ DURING READING:

✏ AFTER READING:

✏ NOTES:

GUIDED READING OBSERVATION NOTES

DATE:
GROUP:

NAMES OF STUDENTS

BEFORE READING	MAKES PREDICTIONS					
	NOTICES NEW WORDS					
	RECOGNISES SIGHT WORDS					
	SCANS TEXT FOR CLUES					
	SCANS IMAGES FOR CLUES					
DURING READING	APPLIES STRATEGIES FOR NEW WORDS					
	READS FLUENTLY					
	SELF-CORRECTS					
	RE-READS FOR MEANING					
AFTER READING	IDENTIFIES MAIN IDEAS					
	SUMMARIZES TOPIC IN ONE SENTENCE					
	RECALLS EVENTS IN PROPER ORDER					
	RETELLS TEXT ACCURATELY					
NOTES						

GUIDED READING PLANBOOK

DATE: _____ GROUP: _____

BOOK TITLE: _____ LEVEL: _____

✏ BOOK INTRODUCTION:

✏ WORD WORK: | ✏ VOCABULARY:

✏ TEACHING STRATEGY:

✏ BEFORE READING:

✏ DURING READING:

✏ AFTER READING:

✏ NOTES:

GUIDED READING OBSERVATION NOTES

DATE:
GROUP:

		NAMES OF STUDENTS				
BEFORE READING	MAKES PREDICTIONS					
	NOTICES NEW WORDS					
	RECOGNISES SIGHT WORDS					
	SCANS TEXT FOR CLUES					
	SCANS IMAGES FOR CLUES					
DURING READING	APPLIES STRATEGIES FOR NEW WORDS					
	READS FLUENTLY					
	SELF-CORRECTS					
	RE-READS FOR MEANING					
AFTER READING	IDENTIFIES MAIN IDEAS					
	SUMMARIZES TOPIC IN ONE SENTENCE					
	RECALLS EVENTS IN PROPER ORDER					
	RETELLS TEXT ACCURATELY					
NOTES						

GUIDED READING PLANBOOK

DATE: _____ **GROUP:** _____

BOOK TITLE: _____ **LEVEL:** _____

✏ BOOK INTRODUCTION:

✏ WORD WORK: | ✏ VOCABULARY:

✏ TEACHING STRATEGY:

✏ BEFORE READING:

✏ DURING READING:

✏ AFTER READING:

✏ NOTES:

GUIDED READING OBSERVATION NOTES

DATE:
GROUP:

		NAMES OF STUDENTS				
BEFORE READING	MAKES PREDICTIONS					
	NOTICES NEW WORDS					
	RECOGNISES SIGHT WORDS					
	SCANS TEXT FOR CLUES					
	SCANS IMAGES FOR CLUES					
DURING READING	APPLIES STRATEGIES FOR NEW WORDS					
	READS FLUENTLY					
	SELF-CORRECTS					
	RE-READS FOR MEANING					
AFTER READING	IDENTIFIES MAIN IDEAS					
	SUMMARIZES TOPIC IN ONE SENTENCE					
	RECALLS EVENTS IN PROPER ORDER					
	RETELLS TEXT ACCURATELY					
NOTES						

GUIDED READING PLANBOOK

DATE: GROUP:

BOOK TITLE: LEVEL:

BOOK INTRODUCTION:

WORD WORK: **VOCABULARY:**

TEACHING STRATEGY:

BEFORE READING:

DURING READING:

AFTER READING:

NOTES:

GUIDED READING OBSERVATION NOTES

DATE: GROUP:	NAMES OF STUDENTS				

BEFORE READING	MAKES PREDICTIONS					
	NOTICES NEW WORDS					
	RECOGNISES SIGHT WORDS					
	SCANS TEXT FOR CLUES					
	SCANS IMAGES FOR CLUES					
DURING READING	APPLIES STRATEGIES FOR NEW WORDS					
	READS FLUENTLY					
	SELF-CORRECTS					
	RE-READS FOR MEANING					
AFTER READING	IDENTIFIES MAIN IDEAS					
	SUMMARIZES TOPIC IN ONE SENTENCE					
	RECALLS EVENTS IN PROPER ORDER					
	RETELLS TEXT ACCURATELY					
	NOTES					

GUIDED READING PLANBOOK

DATE: GROUP:

BOOK TITLE: LEVEL:

✎ BOOK INTRODUCTION:

✎ WORD WORK: ✎ VOCABULARY:

✎ TEACHING STRATEGY:

✎ BEFORE READING:

✎ DURING READING:

✎ AFTER READING:

✎ NOTES:

GUIDED READING OBSERVATION NOTES

DATE:
GROUP:

	NAMES OF STUDENTS				
BEFORE READING					
MAKES PREDICTIONS					
NOTICES NEW WORDS					
RECOGNISES SIGHT WORDS					
SCANS TEXT FOR CLUES					
SCANS IMAGES FOR CLUES					
DURING READING					
APPLIES STRATEGIES FOR NEW WORDS					
READS FLUENTLY					
SELF-CORRECTS					
RE-READS FOR MEANING					
AFTER READING					
IDENTIFIES MAIN IDEAS					
SUMMARIZES TOPIC IN ONE SENTENCE					
RECALLS EVENTS IN PROPER ORDER					
RETELLS TEXT ACCURATELY					
NOTES					

GUIDED READING PLANBOOK

DATE:
BOOK TITLE:

GROUP:
LEVEL:

✏ BOOK INTRODUCTION:

✏ WORD WORK: | ✏ VOCABULARY:

✏ TEACHING STRATEGY:

✏ BEFORE READING:

✏ DURING READING:

✏ AFTER READING:

✏ NOTES:

GUIDED READING OBSERVATION NOTES

DATE:
GROUP:

		NAMES OF STUDENTS				
BEFORE READING	MAKES PREDICTIONS					
	NOTICES NEW WORDS					
	RECOGNISES SIGHT WORDS					
	SCANS TEXT FOR CLUES					
	SCANS IMAGES FOR CLUES					
DURING READING	APPLIES STRATEGIES FOR NEW WORDS					
	READS FLUENTLY					
	SELF-CORRECTS					
	RE-READS FOR MEANING					
AFTER READING	IDENTIFIES MAIN IDEAS					
	SUMMARIZES TOPIC IN ONE SENTENCE					
	RECALLS EVENTS IN PROPER ORDER					
	RETELLS TEXT ACCURATELY					
NOTES						

GUIDED READING PLANBOOK

DATE:

BOOK TITLE:

GROUP:

LEVEL:

✏ BOOK INTRODUCTION:

✏ WORD WORK:

✏ VOCABULARY:

✏ TEACHING STRATEGY:

✏ BEFORE READING:

✏ DURING READING:

✏ AFTER READING:

✏ NOTES:

GUIDED READING OBSERVATION NOTES

DATE:
GROUP:

		NAMES OF STUDENTS				
BEFORE READING	MAKES PREDICTIONS					
	NOTICES NEW WORDS					
	RECOGNISES SIGHT WORDS					
	SCANS TEXT FOR CLUES					
	SCANS IMAGES FOR CLUES					
DURING READING	APPLIES STRATEGIES FOR NEW WORDS					
	READS FLUENTLY					
	SELF-CORRECTS					
	RE-READS FOR MEANING					
AFTER READING	IDENTIFIES MAIN IDEAS					
	SUMMARIZES TOPIC IN ONE SENTENCE					
	RECALLS EVENTS IN PROPER ORDER					
	RETELLS TEXT ACCURATELY					
NOTES						

GUIDED READING PLANBOOK

DATE:
BOOK TITLE:

GROUP:
LEVEL:

✏ BOOK INTRODUCTION:

✏ WORD WORK:

✏ VOCABULARY:

✏ TEACHING STRATEGY:

✏ BEFORE READING:

✏ DURING READING:

✏ AFTER READING:

✏ NOTES:

GUIDED READING OBSERVATION NOTES

DATE:
GROUP:

NAMES OF STUDENTS

BEFORE READING	MAKES PREDICTIONS					
	NOTICES NEW WORDS					
	RECOGNISES SIGHT WORDS					
	SCANS TEXT FOR CLUES					
	SCANS IMAGES FOR CLUES					
DURING READING	APPLIES STRATEGIES FOR NEW WORDS					
	READS FLUENTLY					
	SELF-CORRECTS					
	RE-READS FOR MEANING					
AFTER READING	IDENTIFIES MAIN IDEAS					
	SUMMARIZES TOPIC IN ONE SENTENCE					
	RECALLS EVENTS IN PROPER ORDER					
	RETELLS TEXT ACCURATELY					

NOTES

GUIDED READING PLANBOOK

DATE:

BOOK TITLE:

GROUP:

LEVEL:

✏ BOOK INTRODUCTION:

✏ WORD WORK:

✏ VOCABULARY:

✏ TEACHING STRATEGY:

✏ BEFORE READING:

✏ DURING READING:

✏ AFTER READING:

✏ NOTES:

GUIDED READING OBSERVATION NOTES

DATE:
GROUP:

		NAMES OF STUDENTS				
BEFORE READING	MAKES PREDICTIONS					
	NOTICES NEW WORDS					
	RECOGNISES SIGHT WORDS					
	SCANS TEXT FOR CLUES					
	SCANS IMAGES FOR CLUES					
DURING READING	APPLIES STRATEGIES FOR NEW WORDS					
	READS FLUENTLY					
	SELF-CORRECTS					
	RE-READS FOR MEANING					
AFTER READING	IDENTIFIES MAIN IDEAS					
	SUMMARIZES TOPIC IN ONE SENTENCE					
	RECALLS EVENTS IN PROPER ORDER					
	RETELLS TEXT ACCURATELY					

NOTES

GUIDED READING PLANBOOK

DATE: _____ GROUP: _____
BOOK TITLE: _____ LEVEL: _____

✏ BOOK INTRODUCTION:

✏ WORD WORK: | ✏ VOCABULARY:

✏ TEACHING STRATEGY:

✏ BEFORE READING:

✏ DURING READING:

✏ AFTER READING:

✏ NOTES:

GUIDED READING OBSERVATION NOTES

DATE:
GROUP:

NAMES OF STUDENTS

BEFORE READING	MAKES PREDICTIONS					
	NOTICES NEW WORDS					
	RECOGNISES SIGHT WORDS					
	SCANS TEXT FOR CLUES					
	SCANS IMAGES FOR CLUES					
DURING READING	APPLIES STRATEGIES FOR NEW WORDS					
	READS FLUENTLY					
	SELF-CORRECTS					
	RE-READS FOR MEANING					
AFTER READING	IDENTIFIES MAIN IDEAS					
	SUMMARIZES TOPIC IN ONE SENTENCE					
	RECALLS EVENTS IN PROPER ORDER					
	RETELLS TEXT ACCURATELY					

NOTES

GUIDED READING PLANBOOK

DATE: GROUP:

BOOK TITLE: LEVEL:

✏ BOOK INTRODUCTION:

✏ WORD WORK: ✏ VOCABULARY:

✏ TEACHING STRATEGY:

✏ BEFORE READING:

✏ DURING READING:

✏ AFTER READING:

✏ NOTES:

GUIDED READING OBSERVATION NOTES

DATE: GROUP:	NAMES OF STUDENTS				
BEFORE READING					
MAKES PREDICTIONS					
NOTICES NEW WORDS					
RECOGNISES SIGHT WORDS					
SCANS TEXT FOR CLUES					
SCANS IMAGES FOR CLUES					
DURING READING					
APPLIES STRATEGIES FOR NEW WORDS					
READS FLUENTLY					
SELF-CORRECTS					
RE-READS FOR MEANING					
AFTER READING					
IDENTIFIES MAIN IDEAS					
SUMMARIZES TOPIC IN ONE SENTENCE					
RECALLS EVENTS IN PROPER ORDER					
RETELLS TEXT ACCURATELY					
NOTES					

GUIDED READING PLANBOOK

DATE: GROUP:

BOOK TITLE: LEVEL:

✏ BOOK INTRODUCTION:

✏ WORD WORK: ✏ VOCABULARY:

✏ TEACHING STRATEGY:

✏ BEFORE READING:

✏ DURING READING:

✏ AFTER READING:

✏ NOTES:

GUIDED READING OBSERVATION NOTES

DATE:
GROUP:

NAMES OF STUDENTS

BEFORE READING	MAKES PREDICTIONS					
	NOTICES NEW WORDS					
	RECOGNISES SIGHT WORDS					
	SCANS TEXT FOR CLUES					
	SCANS IMAGES FOR CLUES					
DURING READING	APPLIES STRATEGIES FOR NEW WORDS					
	READS FLUENTLY					
	SELF-CORRECTS					
	RE-READS FOR MEANING					
AFTER READING	IDENTIFIES MAIN IDEAS					
	SUMMARIZES TOPIC IN ONE SENTENCE					
	RECALLS EVENTS IN PROPER ORDER					
	RETELLS TEXT ACCURATELY					

NOTES

GUIDED READING PLANBOOK

DATE: GROUP:

BOOK TITLE: LEVEL:

✎ BOOK INTRODUCTION:

✎ WORD WORK: ✎ VOCABULARY:

✎ TEACHING STRATEGY:

✎ BEFORE READING:

✎ DURING READING:

✎ AFTER READING:

✎ NOTES:

GUIDED READING OBSERVATION NOTES

DATE:
GROUP:

		NAMES OF STUDENTS				
BEFORE READING	MAKES PREDICTIONS					
	NOTICES NEW WORDS					
	RECOGNISES SIGHT WORDS					
	SCANS TEXT FOR CLUES					
	SCANS IMAGES FOR CLUES					
DURING READING	APPLIES STRATEGIES FOR NEW WORDS					
	READS FLUENTLY					
	SELF-CORRECTS					
	RE-READS FOR MEANING					
AFTER READING	IDENTIFIES MAIN IDEAS					
	SUMMARIZES TOPIC IN ONE SENTENCE					
	RECALLS EVENTS IN PROPER ORDER					
	RETELLS TEXT ACCURATELY					
	NOTES					

GUiDED READiNG PLANBOOK

DATE: GROUP:

BOOK TiTLE: LEVEL:

✏ BOOK iNTRODUCTiON:

✏ WORD WORK: ✏ VOCABULARY:

✏ TEACHiNG STRATEGY:

✏ BEFORE READiNG:

✏ DURiNG READiNG:

✏ AFTER READiNG:

✏ NOTES:

GUIDED READING OBSERVATION NOTES

DATE:
GROUP:

	NAMES OF STUDENTS				
BEFORE READING					
MAKES PREDICTIONS					
NOTICES NEW WORDS					
RECOGNISES SIGHT WORDS					
SCANS TEXT FOR CLUES					
SCANS IMAGES FOR CLUES					
DURING READING					
APPLIES STRATEGIES FOR NEW WORDS					
READS FLUENTLY					
SELF-CORRECTS					
RE-READS FOR MEANING					
AFTER READING					
IDENTIFIES MAIN IDEAS					
SUMMARIZES TOPIC IN ONE SENTENCE					
RECALLS EVENTS IN PROPER ORDER					
RETELLS TEXT ACCURATELY					

NOTES

GUiDED READiNG PLANBOOK

DATE: GROUP:

BOOK TiTLE: LEVEL:

✏ BOOK iNTRODUCTION:

✏ WORD WORK: ✏ VOCABULARY:

✏ TEACHiNG STRATEGY:

✏ BEFORE READiNG:

✏ DURiNG READiNG:

✏ AFTER READiNG:

✏ NOTES:

GUIDED READING OBSERVATION NOTES

		NAMES OF STUDENTS				
DATE: GROUP:						
BEFORE READING	MAKES PREDICTIONS					
	NOTICES NEW WORDS					
	RECOGNISES SIGHT WORDS					
	SCANS TEXT FOR CLUES					
	SCANS IMAGES FOR CLUES					
DURING READING	APPLIES STRATEGIES FOR NEW WORDS					
	READS FLUENTLY					
	SELF-CORRECTS					
	RE-READS FOR MEANING					
AFTER READING	IDENTIFIES MAIN IDEAS					
	SUMMARIZES TOPIC IN ONE SENTENCE					
	RECALLS EVENTS IN PROPER ORDER					
	RETELLS TEXT ACCURATELY					
NOTES						

GUIDED READING PLANBOOK

DATE: _____ GROUP: _____
BOOK TITLE: _____ LEVEL: _____

✏ BOOK INTRODUCTION:

✏ WORD WORK: | ✏ VOCABULARY:

✏ TEACHING STRATEGY:

✏ BEFORE READING:

✏ DURING READING:

✏ AFTER READING:

✏ NOTES:

GUIDED READING OBSERVATION NOTES

DATE:
GROUP:

NAMES OF STUDENTS

BEFORE READING	MAKES PREDICTIONS					
	NOTICES NEW WORDS					
	RECOGNISES SIGHT WORDS					
	SCANS TEXT FOR CLUES					
	SCANS IMAGES FOR CLUES					
DURING READING	APPLIES STRATEGIES FOR NEW WORDS					
	READS FLUENTLY					
	SELF-CORRECTS					
	RE-READS FOR MEANING					
AFTER READING	IDENTIFIES MAIN IDEAS					
	SUMMARIZES TOPIC IN ONE SENTENCE					
	RECALLS EVENTS IN PROPER ORDER					
	RETELLS TEXT ACCURATELY					
NOTES						

Made in United States
North Haven, CT
15 August 2022